British Library Cataloguing-in-Publication Data
A CIP record for this title is available from the British Library

ISBN 978 1 84114 888 5

HALSGROVE
Halsgrove House,
Ryelands Industrial Estate,
Bagley Road, Wellington, Somerset TA21 9PZ
Tel: 01823 653777   Fax: 01823 216796
email: sales@halsgrove.com

Part of the Halsgrove group of companies
Information on all Halsgrove titles is available at: www.halsgrove.com

Printed and bound by Grafiche Flaminia, Italy

INTRODUCTION

To many people Carmarthenshire is that bit of somewhere they pass through on their way to and from Pembrokeshire for their holidays. It becomes not so much a place to stop and explore as a 'somewhere' en route. This is such a shame as they do not know what they are missing. Carmarthenshire or, to give its Welsh name, Sir Caerfyrddin (often shortened to Sir Gar), is a county rich in the diversity of its landscapes and attractions.

Carmarthenshire has always been a large county and indeed, up to 1974 was the largest in Wales. In 1974, following a drastic set of boundary and authority changes throughout Wales, the county disappeared, or perhaps it is better to say was swallowed up into the new county of Dyfed, comprising what were previously Carmarthenshire, Pembrokeshire and Cardiganshire. Coming from Pembrokeshire I well remember the controversy that this caused! In 1996 this was all revised once more and Carmarthenshire reappeared as a county and unitary authority to remain (so far) as we know it today.

Stretching from the south Wales coastline up into the Cambrian Mountains the range of landscapes within Carmarthenshire's boundary is truly astounding. The coast, which runs from just east of Llanelli to just west of Pendine, is for the most part flat. It is a coast of sand dunes and estuaries with the occasional cliff outbreak, and is home to the resorts of Pembrey Country Park and Pendine Sands. The rivers Lougher, Tywi and Taf have great wide estuaries surrounded by marshland. Laugharne, with its famous association with Dylan Thomas, is a fascinating and absorbing small town in its own right.

By way of contrast, as we travel north away from the coast, we are first met by a very rich countryside, primarily based on agriculture (not for nothing is the county sometimes referred to as the Garden of Wales). The Twyi Valley is a beautiful part of Carmarthenshire, with wonderful lush rural landscapes. Further up the valley narrows, taking us to the stunning upland landscapes around Llyn Brianne. A turn to the east takes us up into the Mynydd Du or Black Mountain, the westernmost region of the Brecon Beacons National Park, and includes the beautiful lake of Llyn y Fan Fach and the impressive fortress of Carreg Cennen. To the west, we soon get tangled up in the remote regions of Brechfa Forest. Head east and we end up in the deep and tangled lanes around Llanboidy and almost end up in the Presceli Hills of Pembrokeshire. Beaches, hills, woodland, forests, waterfalls and castles. There is an incredible range of places to visit (and photograph!) and explore in Carmarthenshire.

I have had a marvellous time, coupled with some great days out, putting together this photographic portfolio of Carmarthenshire and really do hope that you will also enjoy my days out! It will inevitably be the case that I will have omitted some places that the reader would have wished me to photograph and for that I apologise in advance. I have, however, travelled many miles to seek to bring you a set of photographs to show and share with you the enormous variety of landscapes and locations in this county in the south west of Wales.

Llandovery Cottage Terrace
A busy market town, Llandovery is full of interest if you search around its back streets.
I love these tightly joined colourful terraced cottages.

Llandovery – Statue of Llewelyn ap Gruffydd

Or, more correctly Llewellyn ap Gruffydd Fychan. Llewelyn was a staunch supported of Owain Glyndwr and suffered a dreadful death at the hands of Henry IV, near the spot where the statue is erected.

Cynghordy Chapel
It made me wonder when this little headstone was last visited by anyone, so remote is the location. I also noted the mixed English and Welsh epitaph.

Cynghordy Chapel
This little chapel is beautifully situated right underneath the Cynghordy Viaduct. Its peaceful, rural setting to me sums up the countryside of Carmarthenshire.

The Post Box Cynghordy
This sad and neglected little red letter box
is embedded in the chapel wall.

Cynghordy Valley
The early morning light beautifully shows the smoke rising from the farm chimney in the valley below.

Cynghordy Viaduct
Taken in early autumn, the viaduct arches are lit by the rising sun.
In the distance is the outline of the Black Mountain, or Mynydd Du.

Cynghordy Viaduct
This Victorian masterpiece has eighteen arches to carry the Heart of Wales line across the Cynghordy Valley.

Cynghordy Viaduct
Ethereal early morning mist shows the
strength of outline of the viaduct.

Carreg Cennen Castle
This has to be one of the most dramatically sited castles in Great Britain, let alone Wales. Situated in the western Brecon Beacons Carreg Cennen looks dramatic from any angle.

Carreg Cennen Castle
The castle sits on a high limestone crag, making it look well nigh impregnable.

Farmland at Carreg Cennen

Surrounding the castle is rich farmland. You may be lucky enough to spot
some of the long horn cattle grazing, from the nearby rare breeds farm.

Abandoned Cartwheels
Sometimes the remnants of old farm artefacts and implements can tell their own story of days long gone.

Falls on the River Sawdde

These falls are on the River Sawdde near the rural community of Llandeusant, beneath the Black Mountain or Mynydd Du.

The Hut in the Woods
Whilst out exploring one winter day I came across this abandoned old hut tucked away in the fields near Llandeusant.

Curious Pig, Llandeusant
This pig seemed so delighted to see me it was as if I was the only person to pass the farm that day.

Bridge Over River Cothi at Abergorlech
This three-arched bridge spans the Cothi River at Abergorlech, in the lower Cothi Valley on the Twyi Cothi Trail.

Top:
Cwrt y Cadno Plaque
The plaque is laid into the front wall of 'Cwrt', telling of the dates when the chapel was built
and rebuilt; neither of which tie in with the date on the chapel itself!

Left:
Cwrt y Cadno Methodist Chapel
Located in the remote rural Cothi Valley. I loved the way the chapel
name has been 'worked' around the windows.

Farmland at Cwrt y Cadno
This scene is so typical of the agricultural landscape of Carmarthenshire between the
coastal belt and the uplands of the Black Mountain and Cambrian Mountains.

Signpost, Cwrt y Cadno
Apart from helping lost souls to re-orientate themselves, this signpost
also throws down a challenge to non Welsh speakers!

Above:
Sheep Feeding, Cothi Valley
It was pouring with rain when I spotted these sheep feeding in a small field,
far too busy to worry about me sneaking up on them with my telephoto lens!

Right:
River Cothi
The upper reaches of the river are quite wild with a number of small waterfalls tumbling over rocks through thick woodland.

Far right:
Bwlch y Rhiw Chapel
This has to be one of the most remote chapels in Carmarthenshire, located on the pass between the
Cothi and Tywi Valleys. Rural Carmarthenshire is all about farmland and chapels, or so it seems.

Countryside Near Llwyn Diried
Lying just below the upland area of north Carmarthenshire this picture shows just how rural and remote the farms are here.

Sheep Rounding at Ffarmers
A typical event in a Carmarthenshire lane, this farmer was bringing his sheep to a field nearer the farm buildings.

Above:
Autumn Woodland, Dinas Rock
There is an exciting path right around Dinas Rock, through oak woods and,
in sections, over large and rough boulders. The scenery is stunning.
The site is managed by the RSPB and is very popular with birdwatchers.

Left:
Doethie Valley in Autumn
Near the confluence of the Doethie and Tywi rivers, this remote location
never fails to give a superb autumn display, especially from the myriad
of silver birches growing hereabouts.

Dinas Wood
Just at that time of year when the bracken starts to turn to autumn gold.

Tree, Dinas Wood
This single tree seems to be growing up into the tangle of other trees.

Above:
River Tywi at Dinas Rock
The infant River Tywi just below Llyn Brianne Reservoir and before being joined by the River Doethie.

Right:
Llyn Brianne Reservoir
This enormous reservoir was built as a 'flow control' for the River Tywi, rather than as a direct source of water. Water is drawn off as needed away downstream at Nantgaredig.

Above:
Sunset Over Llyn Brianne
There was a moodiness about this scene that I loved – the remoteness
and solitude somehow seem magnified in evening light.

Left:
Llyn Brianne Reservoir
The reservoir is surrounded by thick forestry plantations and
provides a good habitat for red kites.

Stream Above Llyn Brianne
There are so many small streams and rivers feeding into the reservoir. I was struck by the shape of the flow and the oak leaves trapped on the wet moss.

Soar y Mynydd Chapel
This truly remote spot is surrounded by thick forest between Llyn Brianne and the Tregaron Mountain Road.
It is amazing to think that such a lonely chapel could ever have had much of a congregation but,
when built, it probably served many small (and now long gone) hill farms.

Above:
Trees at Soar y Mynydd
Just five minutes before I took this shot the sky was blue! The silhouettes stand out well against the bright and stormy looking background.

Left:
Soar y Mynydd in Autumn
Surrounded by enormous beech trees there is always a wonderful autumn display here.

Above:

Tywi Estuary near Ferryside

On the day I visited Ferryside the sides of the estuary were crusted with sea ice. The temperature stayed below freezing all day but what great photographic opportunities presented themselves.

Left:

River Tywi Near Soar y Mynydd

A little further north of the chapel the river runs over a shelf in the rock. The walk to this spot is unbelievably boggy!

Llanstephan Castle
The view from across the estuary at
Ferryside really shows the prominent
position on which this castle was sited.

Llanstephan
This pretty estuaryside village is fronted by a vast expanse of unbroken beach.

St Ishmael's Church, Ferryside
This stunning little church must command one of the most dramatic views from a church anywhere in Wales.

St Ishmael's Church, Sundial
Situated above the church door the accuracy of this sundial is spot on. I even checked it against the time setting on the camera, and, yes, it was correct.

Fisherman Statue, Ferryside
This fascinating sculpture sits right in the middle of the village.

Tywi Estuary From Llanstephan Castle
From this high viewpoint the enormity of the estuary can be truly appreciated.

Kidwelly Castle Gatehouse
Surely one of the most underrated castles in Wales, if not the UK, Kidwelly (Cydweli in Welsh) stands out high and proud over the town of Kidwelly and the Gwendraeth River.

Kidwelly Castle Reflected
Photographed on a cold and frosty morning, with the reflection of the castle caught in the waters of the River Gwendraeth below.

Kidwelly Castle from the Gwendraeth
This angle shows the steepness of the slope up to what seems an impenetrable fortress above.

River Gwendraeth and Rainbow
I had enjoyed a superb day out with the camera and this, the icing on the cake, was the last shot of the day
(and, yes, it did pour with rain immediately after I took the picture).

Boathouse on the Taf Estuary at Laugharne
Laugharne is one of my favourite villages, and not just because of the Dylan Thomas connection.
The location on the edge of a wide marshy estuary adds a certain wildness on a changeable winter day.

Boathouse Framed by Rainbow
Standing in a marsh, slowly sinking in the mud
when I took this shot, I was so lucky to have been
at the right place at the right time.

Coastal Marshland
The creeks change dramatically on the changes of the tide, from navigable streams to muddy trenches.

Abandoned Boats on the Marsh
This typifies the point where village meets marshland;
abandoned old boats left to their own devices by the side of narrow, muddy creeks.

High Tide on the Taf Estuary
One lonely boat, moored and seemingly being guarded by a vigilant seagull.

Laugharne Castle
Starting life as a defensive fort, the castle ended up more as a mansion house, and is now completely empty and in ruins.

Laugharne Cobbled Street 1 and Laugharne Cobbled Street 2
The same viewpoint taken on two different days. Rain can be difficult to photograph in but here it really showed off the cobbles to their best.

Laugharne After Rain
The lighting here really appealed to me, enhanced by the
reflection on the shiny, wet pavements.

Laugharne Old Town Hall
The black sky was testament to the mixed bag of weather that was thrown at me on this day but the sun shining through really adds drama to this wonderful building.

Above:
Laugharne Village Cross
Not as old as it looks at first glance, the cross sits in the 'centre' of the village, by the pubs and shops.

Left:
Laugharne Old Town Hall
After the sun, the rain as the old song has it. The lighting had changed completely in about five minutes, giving a totally different picture.

Llanddarog Church
When the old A48 road ran through the little village of Llanddarog, the church and pub here formed a 'mental milestone' for a small boy on a long journey. Nowadays, all is peaceful in Llanddarog.

Llanddarog Church
The chunkiness of the tower and steeple of the church are unusual and can be seen for miles around.

**Countryside
Around Llanddarog**
This is rural Carmarthenshire, the area being given over mainly to agriculture. The view here is to the north from the churchyard.

Above:
The White Hart Barrels
These barrels add a touch of interest to a pub already brimming with nooks and crannies.

Left:
The White Hart
This wonderful thatched pub is known and loved by many, including my father when we were en route to Pembrokeshire 'in the old days'.

Llanelli National Wetlands Centre

This fascinating centre at Penclacwydd, near Llanelli, provides a great day out for those who love seeing nature up close or just going for an interesting walk. The site borders the edge of the Lougher Estuary and has footpaths for all ages and abilities.

Sir Peter Scott
One of the founders of the Worldwide Fund for Nature, Peter Scott was a key driving force in the founding of wetland habitats in the UK, the first being Slimbridge. His bust meets you at the Llanelli Centre reception area.

Pine Tree, Llanelli Wetlands Centre
On my way out I spotted this curiously kinked pine tree in the car park.

Mudflats – Llanelli Old Harbour
Llanelli docklands is currently undergoing a significant investment in new housing and landscaping. This shot captures the mudflats and one of the abandoned boats that still lie on the mud. Its fate is yet to be decided, I guess.

Llanelli Docklands New Housing Development
These apartments have only recently been completed alongside one of the old docks
and must be a stark contrast to the old industrial dockland landscape.

Millennium Coastal Path Visitor Centre and Coastline
The new path has been built from Lougher to Pembrey and is well serviced by the new, modern Visitor Centre.
The path is 22 kilometres long and incorporates a cycleway.

Millennium Coastal Path Visitor Centre
Modern and clean architectural lines make this new addition to the Llanelli waterfront stand out.

Parc y Scarlets Rugby Stadium
The replacement for the world famous Stradey Park, the stadium was still having finishing touches added to it.
(I wonder did the Scarlets beat the Barbarians?).

Parc y Scarlets Pitch
Still in pristine condition when I photographed it. Note the height of the rugby posts!

Above:
Carmarthen Bay Power Station Memorial
You would never know it but just to the east of Burry Port once stood Carmarthen Bay Power Station. This memorial stone, on the Millennium Path, reminds folk of its presence.

Left:
Burry Port and Gower
The site of recent considerable investment, Burry Port is now a busy and popular marina, although not so long ago it was very much an industrial dockland. The beach in the middle background is Whitford Sands on Gower.

Burry Port and Rainbow
The new marina, built around and within the old docks.

Burry Port Beach Before Storm
Photographed into the setting sun, this was the light which preceded a torrential downpour with thunder and lightning all around.

Left:
Pine Trees, Pembrey Country Park
Monterey pine trees cover much of the Park hiding the mass of sand dunes.

Right:
Cefn Sidan Beach
This enormous stretch of sand (pronounced Cevn Sheedan) fronts the Park and offers miles of sandy beach and stunning views across to the Gower Peninsula.

Left:
Cefn Sidan Sands and Big Sky
The one thing that cannot escape your notice here is the sheer enormity of the sky.

Right:
Pembrey Country Park – Anchors
A nearby information panel tells that these anchors were found on the beach at a low tide and are believed to have come from a ship of around 1,000 tons. A big ship indeed for the period of these anchors. The woodwork around the anchors seeks to represent the wreck.

**Pendine Beach
Between Showers**
The lighting on the beach was some of the most dramatic I have seen. I had stopped at the café for a coffee when the sky darkened, the low sun shone across the sands and I dashed for my camera.

Pendine Beach
Looking west towards Dolwen Point
and the Point Café (where eventually
I did manage to drink my coffee).

Cave and Cliffs at Dolwen Point
I had absolutely no idea what lay on the far side of the Point and was astounded to come across these limestone caves and sculptures in the cliffs. The way the rock ran out from the base of the cliff, partly covered by sand, reminded me of a dinosaur's skeletal foot.

Top:
Carmarthen Dragon
This steel dragon was actually being erected on the roundabout at
the end of the footbridge on the last visit I made to Carmarthen.

Left:
Footbridge over the Tywi River, Carmarthen
This dramatic footbridge crosses the river just below the castle and town hall of Carmarthen.

Left:
Carmarthen Guildhall
A well known landmark to those who frequent Carmarthen.

Right:
Lammas Street, Carmarthen
A busy shopping street with shops, cafés, pubs, chapels and churches all happily intermixed.

The Coffe Pot and the Top Hat, Carmarthen
These two symbols of what once went on beneath them were once very popular. They are easy to miss as we seldom take time to look above us when walking through towns.

The Boars, Ammanford
This set of metal statues of the Twrch Trwyth wild boar and her piglets greets you just as you enter Ammanford. They originate from the story about King Arthur chasing the boar across this part of the world.

The Cottage Inn, Ammanford

Once a busy mining village, Ammanford is now a quiet town in the Amman Valley.
This row of cottages has been restored and houses a pub, a kebab house and a café.

Top:
Robin Singing
As if to reinforce the spring message this cheeky
robin sang his heart out in a nearby bough.

Left:
Middleton Hall and Daffodils
Spring at The National Botanic Gardens of Wales is
announced by a mass of miniature (natural) daffodils.

Top:
Paxton's Tower
In the care of the National Trust, the tower contains a banqueting hall,
and a space for carriages to draw up underneath.
Right:
Paxton's Tower, Near Llanarthne
This imposing folly was built on the orders of William Paxton
on the Middleton Hall Estate and dedicated to Lord Nelson.
It commands superb views both up and down the Tywi Valley.

Chickens Heading Home
Llanarthne. On the lane leading down from Paxton's Tower were these hens,
obviously not taught to walk on the right and face oncoming traffic.

Dryslwyn Castle
Not only a castle but also the remains of a medieval village are to be found at
the top of the knoll. Below meanders the Tywi River.

Graveyard at Gelli Aur
Gelli Aur (or Golden Grove) is normally thought of as being the nearby mansion.
But there is also a small village and church, in which lie these headstones, guarded by enormous fir trees.

Wind Damage at Gelli Aur
The weather had been filthy before I passed here. This large tree was brought down
by fierce winds onto the roof of the old school building next to the church.

Autumn Beech Trees at Dynefwr
The woods here change so markedly with the seasons. This was a very overcast and dull day which brings out the colour of the tree trunks to best advantage.

Spring Bluebell Woods at Dynefwr
Spring brings a whole new palette of colours, the bluebells a rich carpet of blue under the light green beech leaves.

Tywi Valley View From Dynefwr Castle
This elevated view shows just what a green and fertile valley this is, with the Tywi River meandering through the middle.

Tywi Valley
This view looks straight down the valley and shows even more the river's meander.
On the left Paxton's Tower can just be made out.

Llandeilo Bridge and Houses
This well known view
encompasses both the bridge,
built around 1845, and the
brightly coloured houses rising up
the hill into the town.

Top:
St Teilo's Church Llandeilo
This unusual view shows the church tower surrounded by old and
seemingly neglected headstones. The main road into Llandeilo in
fact cut through the middle of the churchyard to align with the
'new' bridge. The original thirteenth-century church was
demolished and rebuilt as part of the process.

Right:
Llandeilo Town
The old market town is full of bright colours
and interesting architecture.

Left:
**Gerwyn's Fruit and
Veg Shop, Llandeilo**
This brightly coloured frontage,
full of fresh fruit and vegetables,
greets you as you climb the hill
over the bridge and into the town.

Right:
**The Old Bank, Llandeilo
(and Plaque)**
This office is the site of an old bank, a
branch of The Black Ox Bank, set up
by David Jones, a cattle drover, in
1799, to safeguard earnings.

Talley Abbey

Or, more properly Talyllychau, was a Premonstratensian Abbey, built in or around 1185 by Rhys ap Gruffydd, the Lord Rhys. Evidence indicates that the abbey was never completed. The abbey sits in a beautiful quiet valley setting in the lower Cothi Valley.

Talley Church

The church of St Michael is right next to the abbey ruins. After falling into disrepair the church was rebuilt in its present form in 1773, much of the building material coming from the abbey ruins.

Old Ash Tree and Talley Church

It is believed that this ash tree is the oldest surviving ash in Britain. Whether it is or not the girth of the trunk is massive, and is estimated to be around 36 feet.

House Talley
This stunning and beautifully coloured house sits near Talley Abbey. Some years ago the owner very kindly invited a group of photographers led by me into the garden for tea! This is a belated thank you to the family.

Ruins of Old House near Newcastle Emlyn

I suspect this may have been a toll house once upon a time. Although in a state of ruin there was still glass in the windows.

Old Boot
This old leather boot was inside the house resting on a toadstool infested log. How old is it? Who owned it?

Left:
Chapel at Cwmhiraeth
Not far from Drefach Felindre this chapel with its beautifully clipped bushes sits in a quiet and secluded valley – real rural Carmarthenshire.

Right:
Old Building near Drefach Felindre
I skidded to a halt when I spotted this. Are they cottages, is it a barn? The blue and yellow together with the rusting tin roof just caught my eye.

Drefach Woollen Mill
This is a working museum which also sells woollen products to the public.

Drefach Woollen Mill - Mill Wheel

I sought to capture the movement of the wheel which was spinning at a good rate.

End of Wool Wrap
Drefach Woollen Mill The end of this large wool wrap made a lovely pattern.

Castle, Newcastle Emlyn
This thirteenth-century Welsh-built castle has the River Tefi on three of its four sides.

Left:
Town Hall Clock
through the castle archway.

Right:
River Teifi Weir
The weir controls the flow of river water into a leat for a nearby mill in Newcastle Emlyn itself.

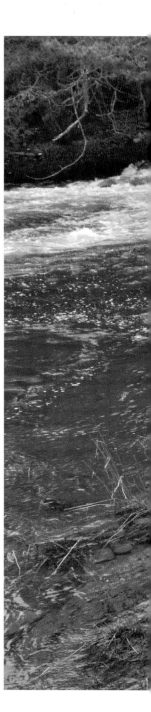

Shops – Newcastle Emlyn
There are many interesting and richly painted shops in this rural market town adding a colourful splash to the High Street.

Shops – Newcastle Emlyn
A traditional butcher with a good Welsh name!

The Pelican Inn, Newcastle Emlyn

Beneath Bannau Sir Gaer
The Black Mountain, or Mynydd Du, is the westernmost section of the Brecon Beacons National Park. The area is remote, beautiful and popular with kites (possibly due to the presence nearby of a kite feeding station near Cross Inn!).

Right:
Llyn y Fan Fach
This jewel of a lake is tucked away under the crest of Bannau Sir Gaer. It is a glacial lake albeit now used as a control for the flow of water in the River Sawdde.

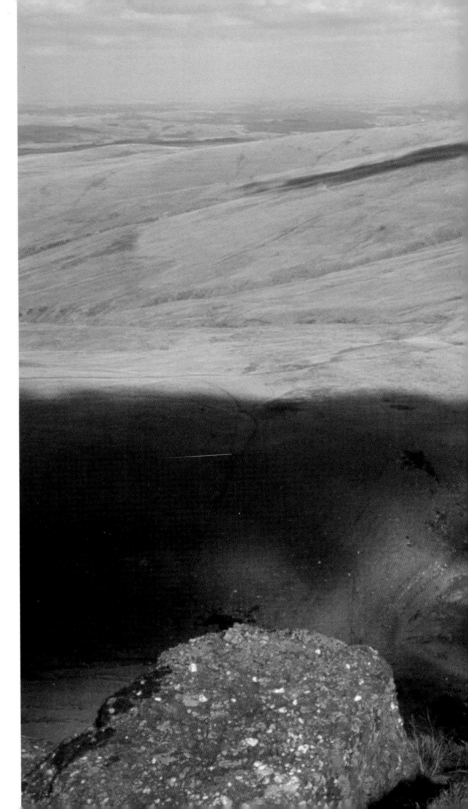

Llyn y Fan Fach

The lake is the location of the ancient story of 'the lady of the lake', involving a local farmer's son, Rhiwallon, and his bid to marry the mysterious lady, who rose from the lake. The theme of the tale, in short, is that she accepted his proposal with the proviso that if he ever struck her three times with iron she, and her dowry, would return to the lake. He did/ she did, but not before leaving him with sons, who, legend has it, went on to become the physicians of Myddfai, doctors who actually existed right up to recent times, specialising in herbal remedies.

Llyn y Fan Fawr
Larger than Llyn y Fan Fach, Llyn y Fan Fawr sits to the east, under the height of Fan Foel.
There is a story that Llyn y Fan Fach has no fish living in it. I have never seen any
but have watched plovers hopping from boulder to boulder here.

Sunset from Brynamman Mountain Road
Coming home one day after photographing Carreg Cennen Castle,
I was confronted with this stunning band of gold across the evening sky.

Loughor Railway Bridge
For those travelling by train this brick-built eleven-arched bridge is either the entry to, or the exit from Carmarthenshire.

Curator's welcome

Logan has long had a reputation for being a plantsman's paradise and has the accolade of being the jewel in the crown of RBGE'S four Gardens, as well as being known as Scotland's most exotic garden.

Since the earliest days of the McDoualls, Logan has always had a reputation for cultivating new and untried species as well as experimenting with new techniques. This tradition continues today, with the plant collection having grown by over 50% during the last 10 years.

Many species are new to cultivation, critically endangered or rarely seen in UK collections. In recent years numerous plants have been acquired following successful plant exploration trips to Chile, the Canaries and latterly Vietnam to further our conservation work overseas.

Logan's benign, mild climate allows plants that are normally grown under glass in the UK to thrive outdoors. The Garden is constantly developing and expanding: the 'green' Victorian-style Conservatory is a real asset and allows us to offer visitors another dimension.

Logan is not just a Garden but also hosts a wide range of events and activities for those seeking a high-quality visitor experience, ranging from jazz and opera nights to children's activities and regular guided walks. In addition, its modern Studio hosts many exhibitions.

In recent years Logan has won the *Dumfries & Galloway Life Awards* 'Tourism Champion of the Year' on two occasions and in 2021 was voted 'Best Garden in the UK' by *Which?* magazine.

We look forward to welcoming you to discover the outstanding wonder that is Logan Botanic Garden.

Richard Baines

Richard A. Baines
Curator, Logan Botanic Garden

Contents

Introduction

Logan estate is on the Rhins of Galloway, the distinctive hammer-head peninsula that juts out into the Irish Sea. The Garden lies 14km north of the southern tip, occupying an area of rolling low ground just 25–40m above sea level. Nestling among low hills in the heart of a farming community, it comprises 10 hectares of woodland enclosing the Walled Garden. Public areas of the Garden take up only 6 hectares, the remainder being used for vital shelterbelt plantations.

Logan enjoys an almost subtropical climate thanks to the warming influence of the Gulf Stream. It receives an average annual rainfall of 1,016mm. In addition, for more than 200 days a year between spring and autumn, the Garden is usually free of air frosts. But these apparently idyllic conditions are frequently shattered by the fierce winds that even on warm summer days can damage the foliage of the more exposed plants, and in winter often exceed 80kph – sometimes reaching 160kph. After a bad winter, salt burn and wind pruning are evident, making the survival of the Garden dependent on its shelterbelt defences.

Dicksonia antarctica (tree fern) against a blue sky.

The Royal Botanic Garden Edinburgh – four Gardens, one Collection

Logan is one of the Regional Gardens of the Royal Botanic Garden Edinburgh (RBGE), four Gardens in Scotland that comprise one of the world's richest collections of plants, containing over 13,000 species from 157 countries and including some that are extinct in the wild and others that are new to science. In 2019 Logan celebrated it's 50th anniversary as part of RBGE, a significant milestone.

The mild climate at Logan allows a focus on plants from the southern hemisphere, especially from Australia and New Zealand, South and Central America, Northern Vietnam and Southern Africa. They constitute a specialised part of RBGE's extensive Living Collection, which is grown and maintained not only for the enjoyment of visitors, but also to support internationally important scientific research, education and conservation.

Botanic gardens play a vital role in modern-day conservation at a time when so many plant species are endangered. Around 472 of the species cultivated at Logan are under threat in the wild. The green conservation boxes throughout this book feature some of the most endangered – and the most beautiful.

The history of the Garden

For over 700 years Logan was in the possession of a single family. In 1295, John Balliol, Lord of Galloway, granted the lands of Logan to Dougal McDouall. In the heart of the estate stand the ruins of Castle Balzieland, the McDouall family's medieval stronghold, which burnt down in around 1500. A new house replaced the castle in 1702, taking the name of Logan, derived from the Gaelic *laggan*, meaning a small hollow. The Walled Garden, incorporating the castle ruins, was constructed around the end of the 18th century as a traditional kitchen garden. For most of the next century Logan remained a traditional, if unremarkable, country house garden.

The original peat walls.

The McDoualls picking lavender.

Kenneth McDouall standing alongside the Himalayan blue poppy.

The present garden dates from 1869 when James McDouall married Agnes Buchan-Hepburn, from Smeaton in East Lothian. She had a great passion for gardening and began to experiment with exotic plantings. Her love of gardening passed to her sons, Kenneth and Douglas, who became expert horticulturists in their own right, travelling widely in warm temperate regions to collect new species and obtaining seed from the expeditions of leading plant collectors of their day. The McDoualls established many of the main structural plantings that define the Garden today.

Kenneth McDouall died in 1945, leaving Logan estate to his cousin, Sir Ninian Buchan-Hepburn. In 1949 the estate passed to Mr R. Olaf Hambro; following his death in 1961, the estate was looked after by a charitable trust until funds became exhausted and the house and gardens were gifted to the nation. In 1969, Sir Ninian reacquired the house and most of its land. The Walled Garden and surrounding woodland became Logan Botanic Garden, a Regional Garden of the Royal Botanic Garden Edinburgh.

Logan was probably the mildest garden in Scotland, but was still too exposed to the destructive blast of the Atlantic gales. The biggest priority throughout the 1970s and 1980s was the building of protective shelterbelts. Martin Colledge had been Head Gardener to the Hambro Trustees and became Logan Botanic Garden's first Curator. Working with the cooperation of scientists and horticulturists in Edinburgh, he began to acquire new, well-documented plants. His successor, Barry Unwin, took over in 1988 and continued to develop the Collections in the spirit of the McDoualls, consolidating Logan's status as the country's most exotic garden. Richard Baines, Curator since 2007, has further developed Logan's status as a true botanic garden.

The Cordyline Avenue

Planting around the Verandah

What to see at the Garden

One visit to Logan will never be enough to explore its vast array of plants, some familiar, most exotic. Here is a guide to the must-see highlights. A walk in the Garden will transport you around the globe and allow you to discover the best of Australia, South America and Southern Africa – all without leaving Scotland.

The Walled Garden – The Walled Garden is divided into smaller gardens, each with its own character, and is a haven for colour and fragrance throughout the season. Look out in particular for the host of brightly coloured borders and unusual climbing plants covering the walls.

Cordyline Avenue – The path to the left of the Walled Garden leads to one of Logan's most iconic – and unmissable – features.

Cabbage Palm Avenue - The entrance driveway, planted in 2015, has nearly 300 cabbage palms creating the longest cabbage palm avenue in the UK.

Lower Walled Garden – Past the Peat Walls, this large area is studded with splendid island beds, each featuring a palm or eucalyptus and a range of brightly coloured plants from the southern hemisphere.

Middle Walled Garden – This sheltered inner garden is a place of seclusion and tranquillity where visitors can rest and admire the beds of rhododendrons, hydrangeas, primulas and many more.

The Woodland Garden – The Woodland Garden encloses the Walled Garden on two sides. A less formal area, it is no less striking, with its collection of eye-catching trees and shrubs with a particular focus on Australasia.

Rhododendron kanehirae

It is thought that this rhododendron is now fully extinct in the wild as a result of flooding of the river banks around its only known locality in northern Taiwan. Even in cultivation, only four plants exist anywhere in the world: RBGE is fortunate to have all four, with two at the Edinburgh Garden and two at Logan. You can spot the bright pink funnel-shaped flowers growing in the Walled Garden.

Conifers

More than one-third of the 630 conifer species in the world are under threat in the wild. RBGE's International Conifer Conservation Programme was set up in 1991 to bring all threatened temperate species into cultivation. A number of species are being nurtured in the Walled and Woodland Gardens, including *Xanthocyparis vietnamensis*, of which fewer than 90 specimens still exist in the wild.

Verandah – The beds on either side of the Verandah are filled with a glorious variety of southern-hemisphere bulbs, corms and salvias.

Castle Woodland – This large area, flanked by the Castle Balzieland ruin, has trees and shrubs from both the northern and southern hemispheres, as well as a fine collection of rhododendrons.

Gunnera Bog – Explore the depths of this strange forest by following the path that leads to the Woodland Pond.

Chile – Rich in wild-collected material from South America, this area leads to the Viewpoint shelter.

Tasmanian Creek – The eucalyptus and tree ferns recreate an antipodean forest habitat in the south-west of Scotland. Use the network of small paths to explore its hidden depths.

Peat Walls – The McDoualls at Logan pioneered the technique of growing plants on peat walls in the 1920s. Since then peat walls have been created around the world. Using terraces of freshly cut peat blocks back-filled with a peaty loam, a specialised environment is created in which plants that prefer moist, acid soil can flourish, in particular Sino-Himalayan plants such as primulas, *Meconopsis*, *Nomocharis*, heaths and rhododendrons.

Eucryphia x *nymansensis* 'Nymansay'.

A slate vase

Cordyline australis

The Logan Conservatory

The Logan Conservatory provides a real focus for exotic plants and offers visitors a haven during periods of inclement weather. It houses a collection of plants from South Africa rarely seen growing on public display in the UK and consolidates Logan's status as Scotland's most exotic garden. The plant collection includes Proteas, tree heathers, a pelargonium collection and tender South African bulbs, allowing Logan to build on its extensive outdoor collection of South African plants, many of which were collected by the eminent botanist Bill Burtt and introduced into cultivation at Logan.

Leucospermum cordifolium

Protea nerifolia

The Conservatory at Logan

The Conservatory at Logan.

Although the building is Victorian in style, its concept is ultra-modern as it uses renewable technologies and is the first entirely carbon-neutral public greenhouse in the UK. The Logan Conservatory is of great educational value as it is envisaged that it will become a centre of innovation for alternative energy and demonstrates at first hand possible alternatives to traditional fossil fuels.

The Discovery Centre

The ideal place to start or end a visit to Logan, the Discovery Centre puts the Garden in context and offers insight into what it is and does. Housed in a picturesque white cottage, more than a century old, which once served as the home of head gardeners and curators, it allows visitors to explore the world of plants and find out more about Logan's past. Interpretation panels and interactive displays help unlock the mysteries of the plant kingdom, while a short film showcases the work of Logan and gives an interesting history of the Garden.

Upstairs, learn more about the work of the Royal Botanic Garden Edinburgh and the world of plants. Downstairs, budding scientists of all ages can examine a specimen under a microscope.

Studio

Created in recent years to house changing exhibitions, with work by local and national artists, this space adds a new dimension for the Logan visitor.

Plants from Australia and New Zealand

Many plants from Australia and New Zealand have been grouped together at Logan, forming an antipodean forest in the Lower South Woodland that gives the visitor a true sense of place, especially in the Tasmanian Creek with its mass plantings of eucalyptus and tree ferns. Natural plant associations are found, such as tree ferns forming an understorey to a collection of eucalyptus trees, or a clematis scrambling through the branches of a *Sophora*.

Eucalyptus

Gum trees, a common term for many species of the *Eucalyptus* genus, are probably among the best-known plants to originate from Australia. Logan grows about 35 species, all of which are recognisable by their pale bluish-green foliage and often beautiful textured bark, such as the snow gum (*E. pauciflora*) which dominates the north-west corner of the Walled Garden.

Tree ferns

Tree ferns are surely the most striking of all antipodean plants at Logan. The majestic but slow-growing *Dicksonia antarctica* can reach up to 12m high in the wild; at Logan the tallest have reached more than 4m and are thought to be more than 150 years old. A more recent addition is *Cyathea dealbata*. If it looks familiar, you may have seen it immortalised on the jerseys of the All Blacks rugby team.

Astelia grandis

Metrosideros umbellata

Callistemon pallidus

Cabbage palms

The cabbage palm – a misnomer as it is not actually a palm – is a common name for *Cordyline australis*, reputedly coined by early settlers in the Antipodes who thought the leaves tasted like cabbage. Cabbage palms were first planted at Logan in 1909 and two other species of *Cordyline* can be found in the Walled Garden: the shrub-like *C. banksii* and the spiky-leaved *C. indivisa*.

Southern rata

New Zealand and Scotland are said to have similar climates, so it is not surprising that several species from New Zealand do well at Logan. Among the most beautiful is the southern rata (*Metrosideros umbellata*), a spectacular woody plant found in the Middle Walled Garden, which has bright-red flowers in July and August.

Bottle brushes

Several species of *Callistemon* are grown at Logan. Looking at the flower spikes, it is easy to see why plants of this genus are commonly known as bottle brushes. Among those grown are the yellow-flowered *C. viridiflorus*, which can be seen in the *Eucryphia* border in the Lower Walled Garden and the Castle Woodland.

Chatham Island forget-me-not

The Chatham Island forget-me-not (*Myosotidium hortensia*) is one of about 50 plants endemic to this tiny archipelago of around ten islands located to the south-east of New Zealand. Its distribution is restricted to coastal habitats. This species is under threat in the wild largely because of grazing by pigs and sheep.

Lobster claw

Lobster claw (*Clianthus puniceus*) is so named because of the distinctive shape of its vivid red flowers. Native to New Zealand, it is now critically endangered in the wild.

Plants from South America

RBGE staff have made several collecting trips to this part of the world, and particularly to Chile, providing Logan with a wealth of beautiful plants that visitors are fortunate enough to be able to admire out of doors.

Chilean highlights

A member of Bromeliaceae, the pineapple family, *Fascicularia canaliculata* ssp. *bicolor* has rosettes of narrow spiny leaves that redden at the base and enclose a compact head of blue flowers in the autumn. From the same family comes the more unusual *Ochagavia carnea*, another stunning bromeliad which you can find on the lower terrace below Castle Balzieland. It produces large pink flower heads in mid-summer. Look out, too, for Chile's national flower, *Lapageria rosea*, a graceful climber that produces beautiful crimson flowers throughout autumn and winter.

Ochagavia carnea

Gunnera

From south-east Brazil comes the giant, rhubarb-like *Gunnera manicata*, one of the largest of the *Gunnera* species. In spring, the plant develops large, cone-shaped flower spikes covered in thousands of tiny greenish flowers. This is followed by the growth of an enormous canopy of barbed leaves up to 2.5m across, raised on stalks up to 3m high. No surprise that with these dimensions it holds the record for producing the largest leaves of any plant that can be grown outdoors in Britain. The Gunnera Bog becomes a virtually impenetrable forest in summer, unless you follow the path through its heart. Near the head of the Rock Gully can be seen the closely related but relatively tiny *G. magellanica*, with leaves a mere 50mm across. At the Peat Walls another six small-leaved species can be found, altogether forming one of our National Plant Collections in association with Plant Heritage.

Filo pastry bark

Instantly recognisable thanks to its distinctive flaking, reddish-brown, papery bark, the Argentinian shrub *Polylepis australis* can be found beside the west wall of the Lower Walled Garden. You may be surprised to know that this dramatic-looking specimen is a member of the rose family and has been reported growing 5,000m above sea level in the Andes, where its layers of bark protect it from the cold.

Jubaea chilensis

The *Jubaea chilensis* (Chilean wine palm) is now only found in the wild in a small area of central Chile. It is a partially protected species in Chile and is under threat largely because of the expansion of land for grazing. The world's largest individual indoor plant specimen is located in the Temperate House in Kew Gardens, and our *Jubaeas* at Logan are seedlings from this.

Juania australis

Also known as the Chonta palm, *Juania australis* is a rare plant endemic to the Juan Fernández Islands west of Chile. A threatened species with very few examples in cultivation outside its native habitat, it is demanding and difficult to grow. It is illegal to export seeds from the Juan Fernández Islands so the example in the Walled Garden is a rare specimen indeed.

Plants from Southern Africa

A number of African genera – especially those grown from bulbs and corms – have species that make excellent garden plants. Look out for the aptly named angels' fishing rods of *Dierama pulcherrimum* around the Pond. Several species and hybrids of *Watsonia* from the lily family bring more late-summer and autumn colour to the Garden, including the *Watsonia pillansii*, with its rich orange flower spikes.

Gladiolus cardinalis (above) – Surely one of the most beautiful of all gladioli, this native of South Africa starts growing in the autumn, produces shoots in winter and finally shows off its magnificent red and white flowers in early summer.

Nerine bowdenii – Named after the Greek mythological sea nymph, the genus *Nerine* belongs to the amaryllis family. Very few of its species can be grown outdoors in British temperatures but *N. bowdenii* thrives at Logan, its strands of pink flowers adding autumn colour to the Walled Garden.

Aloe polyphylla
This striking member of the genus *Aloe* is endemic to mountainous regions of Lesotho in southern Africa, where the climate is cool with a high level of rainfall. A protected species, it is threatened with extinction largely because of illegal collecting, as it is much prized for its ornamental value.

Plants from the Atlantic islands

In the northern hemisphere, warm temperate Islands such as Madeira and the Canaries have a climate that is not dissimilar to that of Logan. These islands may be small, but they are floristically rich and have brought more than a touch of colour to the Garden.

Pride of Madeira – The Atlantic islands' greatest contributions to the Garden are various *Echium* species, several of which flower well here. *E. candicans* is a large perennial commonly known as Pride of Madeira and justifiably so. It produces masses of vivid purple-blue flower spikes in early summer.

Canary spurge – A shrub native to Madeira, the Canary spurge (*Euphorbia mellifera*) grows up to 2m tall and produces honey-scented flowers in spring.

The Irish rose – *Aeonium arboreum* may be commonly known as the Irish rose, but it hails from the Canary Islands. This evergreen succulent has striking rosettes of bright-green leaves. Look out for it in the desert border or at the entrance to the Walled Garden.

Isoplexis sceptrum
A striking endemic from the small island of Madeira is the *Isoplexis sceptrum*, now rarely seen in the wild. A member of the *Digitalis* (foxglove) family, it is known commonly as the Madeira foxglove. Its orange spikes can be seen on the upper level of the Terrace.

Plants from Northern Vietnam

Following several successful expeditions in recent years, new plants have been introduced from the mountains of Northern Vietnam. Many of these plants are classified as endangered and are only found in fragile, sparse populations that are highly threatened. To date, over 30 taxa of rhododendrons and many species of *Schefflera*, *Magnolia* and *Polyspora* have been introduced into the Garden. Five plant species that are new to science have been discovered and it is highly likely that as the collections mature there will be others to follow.

Schefflera macrophylla
Often called the 'Daddy of all Scheffleras' this plant has hand-shaped leaves up to 1.5 metres across and makes an impressive architectural plant in any collection.

Rhododendron tephropeploides
A newly described species with much larger flowers than *R. tephropeplum*, with a wonderful mahogany coloured bark that improves with age.

Polyspora longicarpa
Closely related to Camellias, the showy poached egg-like flowers of *Polyspora longicarpa* normally last all winter at Logan, making it a valuable plant for extending the flowering season.

Logan's natural history and environmental sustainability

The landscape of Logan may be mostly man-made, but it is rich in natural history because the diverse exotic flora creates a range of micro-habitats that can support a whole host of animal and plant life.

In recent years a bioblitz was carried out to gain a snapshot of the flora and fauna found at Logan with six new plants recorded for Wigtownshire vice county, our geographical area for biological recording. In total we found 108 species of bryophytes, 81 species of ferns and flowering plants, 35 bird species and 14 species of butterflies and moths. Logan's clean fresh air allows more than 130 species of lichen to flourish on the rocks and trees, along with more than 60 mosses and 9 liverworts. A new lichen trail has also been installed at the Garden which is supported by a leaflet highlighting the diversity of lichen species growing at Logan.

We take our environmental footprint very seriously and in recent years we have transformed the way the Garden operates. In 2015 we built the first carbon neutral public conservatory in the UK, powered by PV Solar panels and air source heat pumps. We have installed electric vehicle charge points in the car park and have a free water-bottle refill point at the entrance to help reduce single use plastics. We are constantly reducing our reliance on fossil-fuel-based machinery and have aspirations to generate additional electricity on site.

Logan through the seasons

The Garden display may reach its glorious peak in high summer but each season brings something new to admire. From the first foliage of spring through the spectacular floral displays of summer and on to the exotic fruits and late-flowering species of autumn, every day at Logan reveals a different combination of colour, fragrance and texture. The mild Atlantic weather means that even in winter it is possible to admire exotic species grown nowhere else in Scotland. Discover something new with each visit and be inspired by this celebration of the changing cycles of the year.

Gladiolus papilio

Fuchsia 'Lady Boothby'

Spring

Banks of daffodils provide a splash of yellow as the Garden opens its gates once again for a new season. Visitors in spring will also have plenty to admire in the spectacular floral displays provided by the magnolias and camellias – the Camellia Walk in the Middle Walled Garden is at its best in spring. Look out, too, for *Magnolia campbellii* ssp. *mollicomata* 'Lanarth', with its burst of flowers. Early-flowering rhododendrons add to the display; one of the finest is *R. edgeworthii*, with its unbeatable combination of fine flowers, beautiful foliage and delicate fragrance. Logan has few plants that are native to the USA, but *Trillium chloropetalum* is surely one of the prettiest, with its carpet of shade-loving deep-red flowers.

Summer

In early summer the air becomes heavy with scent as more rhododendrons burst into bloom and nectar oozes from the vibrant scarlet flowers of the southern rata. The exotic foliage of the tree ferns and cabbage palms mingles with the wealth of spectacular flowering plants to make Logan a true garden-lover's paradise. Colourful borders line the paths of the Walled Garden and more than 30 species of fuchsia come into flower. Look out, too, for the brilliant display provided by the orange, red and yellow candelabra primulas. The *Gladiolus papilio*, with its delicate pale purple flowers, can be seen in the beds around the Pond, while the elegant pale-orange flowers of the *Hedychium spicatum*, a member of the ginger family, provide another flush of summer colour in the perimeter border.

Agapanthus 'Headbourne hybrid'

Nerine bowdenii under cabbage palms.

Autumn

Logan's mild climate ensures that the warmth of summer extends well into the autumn months, with plenty of colour still in the Garden for visitors to enjoy. Among the highlights of this season are the lily-like flowers of the South African *Nerine*, in bloom throughout the autumn months. Look out, too, for stands of *Agapanthus*, another South African native, near the Verandah, with their vivid blue bell-shaped flowers. The climber *Berberidopsis corallina*, a native of Chile, shows off its delicate crimson bells on the centre wall, while the Australian *Dianella intermedia*'s bright purple berries provide a flash of colour throughout autumn.

Winter

Much of the Garden hibernates in winter, while the staff busy themselves preparing for the new growing season. Extreme winter weather is infrequent here but occasional snowfalls create a landscape that is almost as spectacular as when the Garden is in full bloom. In the Tasmanian Creek, *Eucalyptus* is at its most beautiful, with its textured trunks showing off markings in a variety of hues. Dark evergreens provide a backdrop to rare splashes of colour. Logan is lucky enough to be able to grow outdoors several species of *Correa*, evergreen shrubs native to Australia and Tasmania. *Correa backhousiana* produces yellow bell-shaped flowers all through the winter season.

Musa ensete 'Ventricosum'

The Pond in winter.

Aeonium arboreum 'Atropurpureum'

Dianella tasmanica

Protea nerifolia

Managing
the collection

The unusual plant collection that greets the visitor to Logan is an echo of the pioneering work carried out by the McDouall brothers. More than that, however, it is a tribute to the team of horticulturists who work in conjunction with nature to plan, cultivate and maintain the collection to create a spectacular display for visitors to enjoy.

Logan in numbers

10 hectares

7 horticultural staff

2 tractors

An average of 20 intern students every year

1,016mm average annual rainfall

1,877 plant species

162 plant families

More than 11,000 trees planted in the shelterbelt

More than 15 species of palms

30 benches

33,000 visitors every year

The first eucalyptus ever to be planted outdoors in Scotland

Conservation at Logan

Carrying out ex-situ conservation is a key priority for RBGE. In recent years it has been an active partner in the International Conifer Conservation Project (ICCP) and more recently contributed towards the Global Conservation Consortium for *Rhododendron* (GCCR). A fine example of this is *Rhododendron kanehirae* which grows well at Logan but is now extinct in the wild.

The IUCN Red List is a critical indicator of the health of the world's biodiversity and is divided into the categories seen in the table below alongside the number of plants corresponding to each in cultivation at Logan.

Logan in numbers	
Extinct in the wild (EW)	3
Critically Endangered (CR)	32
Endangered (EN)	58
Vulnerable (VU)	71
Near Threatened (NT)	125
Least Concern (LC)	694
Data Deficient (DD)	31

Text © Royal Botanic Garden Edinburgh, 2016

Reprinted 2022

ISBN: 978-1-910877-08-1

Images by Peter Clarke, Gerry Ewan, Janice Gibson, Chris Johnston,
Peter Middleton, Jackie Paddison, Polly Pullar and Brenda White

Text by Anna Stevenson, Richard Baines, Colin Belton and Anne Ramsay

Design and layout by Caroline Muir

The Royal Botanic Garden Edinburgh is a Non Departmental Public Body (NDPB) sponsored and supported
through Grant-in-Aid by the Scottish Government's Environment and Forestry Directorate (ENFOR).
The Royal Botanic Garden Edinburgh is a Charity registered in Scotland (number SC007983).

All information correct at time of going to press.

Printed by Ivanhoe Caledonian Printing Company Ltd